Biblical Foundation 12

The Great Commission

by Larry Kreider

House To House Publications
Lititz, Pennsylvania USA

The Great Commission

Larry Kreider

Updated Edition © 2002, Reprinted 2003, 2007
Copyright © 1993, 1997, 1999
House to House Publications
11 Toll Gate Road, Lititz, PA 17543
Telephone: 800.848.5892
Web site: www.dcfi.org

ISBN 10: 1-886973-11-3
ISBN 13: 978-1-886973-11-4
Design and illustrations by Sarah Sauder

C O N T E N T S

Books in this Series

This is the twelfth book in a twelve-book series designed to help believers to build a solid biblical foundation in their lives.

1 **Knowing Jesus Christ as Lord**
   God's purpose for our lives through a personal relationship with Jesus

2 **The New Way of Living**
   True repentance and faith toward God

3 **New Testament Baptisms**
   Four baptisms including baptism in water and baptism in the Holy Spirit

4 **Building For Eternity**
   The hope of the resurrection, the laying on of hands and eternal judgment

5 **Living in the Grace of God**
   Applying God's grace to everyday living

6 **Freedom from the Curse**
   Christ brings freedom to every area of our lives

7 **Learning to Fellowship with God**
   How to deepen our relationship with Jesus Christ

8 **What is the Church?**
   Finding our place in God's family

9 **Authority and Accountability**
   How to respond to leadership and fellow believers God places in our lives

10 **God's Perspective on Finances**
   How God wants His people to handle money

11 **Called to Minister**
   Every Christian's call to serve

12 **The Great Commission**
   Our purpose for living on this planet

A corresponding *Biblical Foundations for Children* book is also available (see page 64).

Introduction

The foundation of the Christian faith is built on Jesus Christ and His Word to us, the Holy Bible. This twelve-book *Biblical Foundation Series* includes elementary principles every Christian needs to help lay a strong spiritual foundation in his or her life.

In this twelfth Biblical Foundation book, *The Great Commission,* we discover that as disciples of Jesus Christ, our marching orders are to go and make disciples. We can start right where we are! God has called us as His church to touch every nation of the world, but we must ask the Lord where He has called us specifically. Although some believers will go to another country to make disciples, many believers will reach out to others right where they live. God places people all around us we can disciple and train.

We will learn what it means to go as a spiritual force (army) to evangelize, make disciples and mentor others and see the kingdom of God advance! We will discover an effective way of making disciples is by mentoring others in a spiritual father or mother capacity. Spiritual fathers and mothers are those who gently help develop and encourage those they mentor to walk the path of becoming spiritual fathers and mothers themselves. This kind of training by mentoring challenges all believers to both have and become spiritual parents, thus producing lasting and far-reaching results. In fact, this entire series of Biblical Foundation books was written to serve as a tool for any believer who is willing and obedient to make disciples according to the plan of our Lord Jesus Christ.

In this book, the foundation truths from the Word of God are presented with modern day parables that help you easily understand the basics of Christianity. Use this book and the other 11 *Biblical Foundation* books to lay a solid spiritual foundation in your life, or if you are already a mature Christian, these books are great tools to assist you in discipling others. May His Word become life to you today.

God bless you!
Larry Kreider

How to Use This Resource

Personal study

Read from start to finish as an individual study program to build a firm Christian foundation and develop spiritual maturity.

- Each chapter has a key verse excellent to commit to memory.
- Additional scriptures in gray boxes are used for further study.
- Each reading includes questions for personal reflection and room to journal at the end of the book.

Daily devotional

Use as a devotional for a daily study of God's Word.

- Each chapter is divided into 7-day sections for weekly use.
- Additional days at the end of the book bring the total number of devotionals to one complete month. The complete set of 12 books gives one year's worth of daily devotionals.
- Additional scriptures are used for further study.
- Each day includes reflection questions and a place to write answers at the end of the book.

Mentoring relationship

Use for a spiritual parenting relationship to study, pray and discuss life applications together.

- A spiritual father or mother can easily take a spiritual son or daughter through these short Bible study lessons and use the reflection questions to provoke dialogue about what is learned.
- Read each day or an entire chapter at a time.

Small group study

Study this important biblical foundation in a small group setting.

- The teacher studies the material in the chapters and teaches, using the user-friendly outline provided at the end of the book.

Taught as a biblical foundation course

These teachings can be taught by a pastor or other Christian leader as a basic biblical foundation course.

- Students read an assigned portion of the material.
- In the class, the leader teaches the assigned material using the chapter outlines at the end of the book.

CHAPTER 1

What is the Great Commission?

KEY MEMORY VERSE

Therefore go and make disciples of all nations,
baptizing them in the name of the Father and
of the Son and of the Holy Spirit,
and teaching them to obey everything I have
commanded you. And surely I am with you always,
to the very end of the age.
Matthew 28:19-20

Go and make disciples

After Jesus had risen from the dead and was ready to go back to His Father in heaven, He called His twelve disciples together and gave them some last minute instructions. We often refer to this as the "Great Commission." We read about it in Matthew 28:18-20, *Then Jesus came to them and said, "All authority in heaven and on earth has been given to me. Therefore go and make disciples of all nations, baptizing them in the name of the Father and of the Son and of the Holy Spirit, and teaching them to obey everything I have commanded you. And surely I am with you always, to the very end of the age."*

Wouldn't you like to have been there when Jesus gave these last minute "marching orders" to His disciples? Even though He would leave them to go to be with His heavenly Father, He promised to be with the disciples to the end.

Their mission on earth would be to make disciples in all nations. Jesus is still giving this commission to us today. As disciples of Jesus Christ, our marching orders are to go and make disciples.

A *commission* is *a set of orders or instructions*. "Going" is not an option with Jesus' instructions to make disciples of all the nations. Some Bible scholars tell us that the word "go" when translated from the original Greek language implies "having gone." In others words, as we live our lives for Jesus Christ, God has already called us to make disciples wherever we are. We may fulfill this call on the job, in our families, in our communities, in the church or on the mission field. Everywhere we go, we are called to make disciples.

In this Biblical Foundation book, *The Great Commission*, we will learn what it means to go as a spiritual force (army) to evangelize, make disciples and mentor others and see the kingdom of God advance! We will discover an effective way of making disciples is by mentoring others in a spiritual father or mother capacity. Spiritual fathers and mothers are those who gently help develop and encourage those they mentor to walk the path of becoming spiritual

REFLECTION
What is a commission? Where are you called to make disciples?

fathers and mothers themselves. This kind of training by mentoring challenges all believers to both have and become spiritual parents, thus producing lasting and far-reaching results. In fact, this entire series of Biblical Foundation books was written to serve as a tool for any believer who is willing and obedient to make disciples according to the plan of our Lord Jesus Christ.

Reach the nations

An important part of the Great Commission is sending missionaries to areas of the world that have never heard the good news of Jesus Christ. There are many groups of people in areas of the world who have never heard the gospel. Christians are commanded by the Lord to reach people from all nations...*therefore go and make disciples of all nations...(Matthew 28:19).*

God has called us as believers in Jesus Christ to carry the gospel to the very ends of the earth. Missionaries are those who have heard the call of God to live out their witness for Jesus within another culture in a region of the world unfamiliar with the gospel. They hear God's heart to carry the news of eternal salvation to those dying without truth. Missionaries want to express their faith in the language of the common person in the country in which they live. They go into a nation, learn to speak the language and live among the people to explain the gospel and love people as they are drawn into the kingdom of God.

A person called to be a missionary wants to see the gospel penetrate the hearts of people and the societies in which they live. As they live in their "adopted" nation, they reach out to those the Lord places in their lives. God is looking for men and women who will go as missionaries to live out their faith in Christ in their new surroundings. Perhaps God will use your life to bring the message of salvation to needy people in another country.

REFLECTION
Where are we commissioned to carry the gospel, according to Matthew 28:19? How can we practically obey the Lord to reach the world?

All of us are called to be involved in missions in some way. Some are called to go while others are called to both pray for missionaries and to support them financially. Ask the Lord to reveal His plan to you regarding world missions.

The strategy

The Great Commission of our Lord Jesus Christ is really very simple. It is a call to make disciples. You may ask, "How do we go to all the world to make disciples?" We start right where we are! God has called us as His church to touch every nation of the world, but we must ask the Lord where He has called us specifically. Although some believers will go to another country to make disciples, many believers will reach out to others right where they live. God places people all around us we can disciple and train.

Disciples are made one at a time. Jesus ministered to multitudes of people, but He spent most of His time with just twelve disciples. Jesus had different levels of relationships among those He ministered to. John was probably Jesus' closest friend, according to John 13:23. John was joined by Peter and James, another circle of intimate friends Jesus had. The rest of the twelve disciples comprised another level of friendships for Jesus. Jesus also spent time with seventy of His disciples as well as with the 120 who witnessed Him ascending to His Father in heaven (Acts 1:15).

REFLECTION
How are disciples made? Think of your spheres of friendships; how can you make disciples within those spheres?

So then, in the same way Jesus had levels of friendships, you will also have various spheres of friendships. The Lord desires for you to walk closely with a few people at a time so that you can "pour your life" into them. The church of Jesus Christ is built through relationships according to 1 Peter 2:5. *You also, like living stones, are being built into a spiritual house....* Each of us is a building stone for God to use in building His kingdom. We are built together and are held together by these God-ordained relationships.

God's intention is to raise up spiritual parents who are willing to nurture spiritual children and help them grow up in their Christian lives. Billy Graham was once asked what he would do if he wanted to impact a city. His plan was simplistic and strategic. He would find a few key men in the city, spend time with them, and literally pour his life into them, training them in the things the Lord had shown him. As their spiritual father, he then would encourage each of these men to do the same—to find other men and to pour their lives into them. This is the essence of discipleship and spiritual parenting. The renowned evangelist believed he could see an entire city affected for Christ through this strategy. I heartily agree. The Lord is bringing back the truth of discipleship and spiritual parenting to the church of Jesus Christ.

Relationships last forever

The Lord has called us to build relationships with one another. Relationships, although they may change, last forever. When you and I get to heaven, all that is really going to count is the relationship we have with God and with one another. Church buildings and church programs will crumble, but relationships last throughout eternity. The early church met "house to house" so they could experience family-type relationships to the fullest. Relationships were the key to the kingdom of God as they met in each others homes to nurture, equip and serve each other. *So continuing daily with one accord in the temple, and breaking bread from house to house, they ate their food with gladness and simplicity of heart, praising God and having favor with all the people. And the Lord added to the church daily those who were being saved (Acts 2:46-47 NKJ).*

New people were continually added to the church family because these early Christians practiced loving one another. They met in small groups so that disciples could be made more easily. More and more churches today utilize small groups because they are a place where everyone's gifts and talents can be exercised and experienced. In small groups, fellow Christians can pray for one another and experience God personally as they obey God's mandate to make disciples.

You see, making disciples does not just happen. Pray and ask God to show you those relationships He desires for you to build so you can "pour your life" into others and help them become mature believers in Jesus Christ. The Word of God has power to transform lives.

I am not ashamed of the gospel, because it is the power of God for the salvation of everyone who believes: first for the Jew, then for the Gentile (Romans 1:16).

For the message of the cross is foolishness to those who are perishing, but to us who are being saved it is the power of God (1 Corinthians 1:18).

The gospel is powerful! Some people have a career of handling dynamite, knowing just how to blow holes in sides of mountains in order to construct roads. The explosive properties of dynamite, when used properly, are quite effective. We can be effective, too, when we realize we can spread the gospel which will be explosive in a positive way in our communities to change lives! During the Welsh Revival of the early 1900's, many police officers had nothing to do; crime had diminished due to the impact of the gospel. The police force instead formed quartets and sang for community functions!

REFLECTION
Why is a small group a more effective setting for discipling than a larger group?

DAY 5 Your life is read like a book

Paul, the apostle, instructed the early believers to follow his lifestyle as he followed Christ. *Imitate me, just as I also imitate Christ (1 Corinthians 11:1 NKJ).*

People will imitate us when our lives imitate a love for God and others. They will be attracted to Jesus because of seeing His character in our lives. Do you know that the only spiritual book that some people ever read is the book of your life? In fact, the Bible says in 2 Corinthians 3:2-3, *You yourselves are our letter, written on our hearts, known and read by everybody. You show that you are a letter from Christ, the result of our ministry, written not with ink but with the Spirit of the living God, not on tablets of stone but on tablets of human hearts.*

In the Old Testament, the laws of God were written on the tablets of stone at Mount Sinai. But now, under the new covenant of Christ, the Holy Spirit writes God's law in people's hearts. This internal law consists of our love for God and others. People "read" our lives like a book. This is a tremendous privilege, because we are modeling the kingdom of God to those around us as people watch our lives.

If you are a parent, people watch how you relate to your children. If nonbelievers play sports with you, you have the privilege of showing them godly attitudes as you play. In your home, workplace, community, or school, people are watching to see if your life really exemplifies the principles of God. If they see you fail or make a mistake, they will hopefully also see you repent and make it right. People are looking for real Christians, not religious people who live by a legalistic set of man-made laws. They are looking for people with the love of God written on their hearts.

My life has been most profoundly changed through watching the example of others who have lived their Christian lives in front of me. Although I have enjoyed reading good books and listening to great preachers, the most powerful impact that Christ has had in my life comes from seeing Him modeled through other believers.

Sometimes those that I've been patterning my life after have made mistakes. But I've also seen their sincere repentance. Their example has spurred me on to "love and good deeds" (Hebrews 10:24). I'm eternally grateful for those the Lord has placed around me to help me grow in my Christian life and be conformed to the image of Jesus Christ.

REFLECTION
Who should we imitate (1 Corinthians 11:1)? Describe a time you saw Christ in someone and it influenced your life.

Minor on differences; major on Jesus

One of the reasons many of God's people have lost sight of making disciples is because the enemy has deceived them, causing them to focus on problems and differences in the church. We need to focus on Jesus and on making disciples. Matthew 6:33 tells us, *But seek first his kingdom and his righteousness....*

God's kingdom is simply the King, Jesus Christ, and His domain. God is the ruler and the King of the whole universe. We are His servants and a part of His domain. His kingdom includes every believer who names the name of Jesus Christ. It includes every congregation and family of churches who honor Him as Lord and believe in His Word.

His kingdom has variety. When I have the opportunity to attend a family reunion, I am amazed at how different each of us looks, even with some common characteristics. Just as each family has its own distinctive characteristics, every congregation, denomination, or family of churches in God's kingdom has its own distinguishing characteristics. Instead of majoring on the differences, the Lord's desire is for us to major on Jesus and the things we can agree on.

For example, some Christians may have a personal conviction as to whether or not they should celebrate certain holidays. We need to be careful that we do not allow these issues to divide us. The Bible tells us, *One man considers one day more sacred than another; another man considers every day alike. Each one should be fully convinced in his own mind (Romans 14:5).*

We need to know what we believe about these minor issues and not be pressured by others into seeing these issues in exactly the same way. We should also be careful not to try to force everyone else to believe as we do on these minor issues.

We are called to join together in unity to build His kingdom. Let's focus on Jesus and on fulfilling His Great Commission. When we get to heaven, we will probably all find out that we were wrong about certain things. It's reassuring to know that Jesus is committed to us, regardless! In Jesus' prayer for believers in John 17:20-21, He prays for their spiritual unity. *My prayer is not for them alone. I pray also for those who will believe in me through their message, that all of them may be one, Father just as you are in me and I am in you. May they also be in us so that the world may believe that you have sent me.*

Our oneness is based on our common relationship to Jesus. We do not have to think exactly alike, but God wants His children to have the same basic attitudes toward God's truth as revealed in His Word. The devil has tried to divide the church of Jesus Christ for generations. Do not allow the devil to use you to criticize His church.

Jesus Christ is coming back for a church who is in love with Him and with one another. Our God is coming back for a spotless bride...*to present her to himself as a radiant church, without stain or wrinkle or any other blemish, but holy and blameless (Ephesians 5:27).*

REFLECTION
What do you think the spotless bride of Christ will look like?

Although the church is far from perfect, we are being conformed into the image of Christ and becoming the spotless bride our Lord Jesus has called us to be.

Prayer, evangelism and discipleship

Jesus' life was characterized by the basic values of prayer, evangelism and discipleship. These basic values characterizing the life of Jesus remind me of a three-legged stool. I live in a farming community. Many of those who have grown up on a farm can remember their parents using a three-legged milking stool to sit on while milking the cows each morning and evening. Why were there only three legs on the stool? Because no matter where you would set the stool on the barn floor, it would always be stable.

In the same way, we believe God has given His church a three-legged stool of truth as He uses prayer, evangelism and discipleship to build His church. When we give our lives to help others by praying for them, reaching out to them and discipling them, the Lord will make sure we are blessed in return. In fact, the greatest way to be blessed is to do what the scripture says in Luke 6:38, *Give, and it will be given to you. A good measure, pressed down, shaken together and running over, will be poured into your lap. For with the measure you use, it will be measured to you.*

Ecclesiastes 11:1 tells us, *Cast your bread upon the waters, for after many days you will find it again.* Taking the time and effort to reach out to disciple and mentor another person may look like you are throwing away your chance for having your own needs met, but by sowing into others' lives, we are promised to reap a return. Proverbs 11:25 says...*he who refreshes others will himself be refreshed.*

A friend once told us about a time she was sick and needed to be healed. Instead of focusing on her own problem, she started to pray for someone else who needed healing. During the prayer, the Lord miracu-

REFLECTION
When we pour our lives out for others, what are we promised in Luke 6:38? In Proverbs 11:25?

lously touched our friend's body and brought healing into her life. As she refreshed someone else, she was refreshed.

CHAPTER 2

Get Ready for Action! Spiritual Warfare

Put on whole armor of God, that you may stand against attack of the devil.

KEY MEMORY VERSE

For our struggle is not against flesh and blood,
but against the rulers, against the authorities,
against the powers of this dark world and against
the spiritual forces of evil in the heavenly realms.
Ephesians 6:11-12

We are a spiritual army

Throughout the scriptures, Christians are exhorted to be spiritual soldiers, fighting in spiritual battles. Imagine how absurd it would be if all you did in the army was go to meetings to learn how to be in the army. True soldiers do more than go to meetings! They have to endure hardship and suffering in the world. *Endure hardship with us like a good soldier of Christ Jesus (2 Timothy 2:3).* They engaged in warfare.

Likewise, in God's kingdom, we are called to be a spiritual army, willing to endure suffering and difficulties as we help other people come out of spiritual darkness into the kingdom of light. The reason Christians get together in small groups or in larger church meetings is to be trained from the Word of God so they can go out into the world as victorious spiritual soldiers. God has called us to help people come to know Jesus Christ.

The church is like an army with a medical unit. If God's soldiers get wounded, they can receive healing and get back on the battlefield. As the church, we can help people come to know Jesus Christ and grow in Him. God is building His kingdom. His kingdom is made up of many different churches, families of churches, and denominations who are called to work together throughout the world.

We must encourage other Christians to continue in the faith...*encourage one another daily...(Hebrews 3:13a).* Let's encourage and strengthen one another so we can stand together as a strong army, preparing for the return of our Lord Jesus. We are called to encourage people every day throughout the body of Christ through cards, letters, phone calls and acts of kindness. The devil lies to God's people

REFLECTION
How often should we encourage each other, according to Hebrews 3:13? How do you encourage others?

by telling them they are no good, that they will never fulfill the Lord's purpose for their lives. God wants us to build His people up and strengthen and encourage them. We counteract the lies of the devil by speaking the truth of God's Word to others and encouraging them.

In this chapter, we will look at the weapons of spiritual warfare the Lord has given us as we accomplish the Great Commission.

Prayer—A spiritual weapon to wage war

Spiritual warfare is real. The spirit world is real. Two major tactics of the enemy are to first make us believe he is not real, and secondly to produce an overemphasis on him. Some people choose to believe the devil is just a fairy tale—a guy in a red costume with pointed ears and a tail. Just because we cannot see the devil does not mean he is not real. We cannot see radar, radio waves or nuclear radioactivity, but they are still very real.

Other people blame everything on demons and the devil. They overemphasize his power instead of the Lord's. We must keep our focus on Jesus, not on the enemy. Sometimes, instead of blaming everything on demons and the devil, there may be an area in our lives the Lord wants to discipline. We must continually war against those things that limit God's work in our lives.

How does a Christian wage war? We must be strong in the Lord and put on the whole armor of God to engage in our spiritual conflict with evil. We wage this spiritual warfare by the power of the Holy Spirit (Romans 8:13). Paul tells us in Ephesians 6:10-12 to put on spiritual armor like a soldier does so we can stand against Satan's schemes. *Finally, be strong in the Lord and in his mighty power. Put on the full armor of God so that you can take your stand against the devil's schemes. For our struggle is not against flesh and blood, but against the rulers, against the authorities, against the powers of this dark world and against the spiritual forces of evil in the heavenly realms.*

Our fight is not with people; the real war is with the demons of hell, the angels of darkness. The only weapons to which they respond are spiritual weapons. Prayer is a powerful spiritual weapon against the powers of darkness. 2 Corinthians 4:3-4a tells us, *And even if our gospel is veiled, it is veiled to those who are perishing. The god of this age has blinded the minds of unbelievers, so that they cannot see the light of the gospel....*

Satan blinds the minds of people who do not believe. Those who do not submit themselves to Jesus are under Satan's rule. He "veils" their eyes to the truth of the gospel to keep them from believing in Jesus Christ. Imagine driving down a road and seeing a sign alerting you that a bridge is washed out. You immediately know you should follow the detour. Now imagine a drunk driver seeing the same sign. With his impaired judgment, he may read the sign without truly comprehending the dangers. It is possible he may drive off the edge of the bridge to his destruction, because he was blinded to the truth. People all around us today are going to hell. The Bible makes it clear that we can pray and bind the powers of darkness in Jesus' name, so that people will see the truth. Matthew 18:18 says, *I tell you the truth, whatever you bind on earth will be bound in heaven, and whatever you loose on earth will be loosed in heaven.*

Jesus says we can bind (tie up spiritually) the demonic strongholds that are in people's lives. There is power in prayer. As we bind these strongholds in Jesus' name, people will be set free to hear the gospel and respond to Jesus Christ.

A young man once told me, "The only reason I am a Christian today is because my mother prayed for me." This mother understood the principles of the kingdom of God.

Let's get serious about praying for those whom the Lord has placed in our lives and who need to draw closer to Jesus. We can bind the blinding spirits deceiving them so that they can understand and respond to the good news of Jesus Christ.

REFLECTION
How do we stand against Satan's schemes (Ephesians 6:10-12)?

Truth keeps you grounded

We saw in Ephesians 6:10-12 that before we wrestle with demonic strongholds (principalities and powers), we need to put on the whole armor of God. The next two verses mention the first piece of armor to put on. *Therefore put on the full armor of God, so that when the day of evil comes, you may be able to stand your ground, and after you have done everything, to stand. Stand firm then, with the belt of truth buckled around your waist...(Ephesians 6:13-14a).*

When Paul, the apostle, was writing this, he was sitting in a prison cell looking at soldiers who surrounded him. He was able to write from a spiritual perspective about what he saw in the natural realm. He was able to stand his ground in his day of trial. Some days may be very easy for you and other days you may find yourself under intense attack from the devil. These attacks may come in the form of depression, oppression, fear or confusion. When the "evil day" comes, we need to learn how to stand as good soldiers of Jesus

Christ. If we do not stand firmly, we will get knocked off our feet. We must stand, having "truth buckled around our waist."

The Bible tells us that Jesus Christ is the way, the truth and the life (John 14:6). The armor and each of the weapons strapped fast to the soldiers guarding Paul in his prison cell were stabilized by a belt. This is why we need to have the spiritual belt of truth in place in our lives. We build everything in our Christian lives on the truth of the Word of God and on the truth of Jesus Christ.

Speak the truth of God's Word every chance you get. Quote the scripture to yourself and to others. Remember, God's truth will set you free.

What covers your heart and feet?

As Christian soldiers, our spiritual armor includes a full suit. Ephesians 6:14b-15 continues on to name more spiritual pieces of armor to put on...*with the breastplate of righteousness in place, and with your feet fitted with the readiness that comes from the gospel of peace.*

Righteousness refers to our *right standing with God,* which comes only by faith in Jesus Christ (Romans 4:3-5). Sometimes, we may see ourselves through the eyes of our own mistakes. However, as we repent and come to the cross, God always sees us as righteous instead of seeing us. He sees His Son, the Lord Jesus, the perfect lamb that was slain. Whenever we have a problem, the enemy will tell us that God is probably punishing us or something is wrong with us. We must stand against the enemy in Jesus' name. We need to know we are righteous through faith in Jesus Christ.

We also need to make sure our feet are fitted with the "readiness that comes from the gospel of peace." The Lord has called us to walk in peace with our God and with all men. The Bible tells us in James 3:18, "Now the fruit of righteousness is sown in peace by those who make peace." We can negotiate life's obstructions more easily if we attempt to live peaceably with others. If peace is broken, it doesn't matter whose fault it is; we are called to be peacemakers and be reconciled to our brothers and sisters in Christ. If we need help, the

Lord has provided the elders of the local church as mediators to help with these kinds of difficulties. We need to be ready and prepared to declare that the gospel of Jesus Christ brings peace with God and peace with our fellow man.

Therefore, if you are offering your gift at the altar and there remember that your brother has something against you, leave your gift there in front of the altar. First go and be reconciled to your brother; then come and offer your gift (Matthew 5:23-24).

If it is possible, as far as it depends on you, live at peace with everyone (Romans 12:18).

The Lord asks us to do all we can to pursue peace with others, and then trust Him to do the rest. Only God can change people's hearts and cause them to be reconciled.

REFLECTION
How do we obtain righteousness? How can you be a peacemaker? Explain.

Hold your shield of faith in place

The piece of armor that a soldier really relied upon was the shield. The soldier's shield was a two foot by four foot shield behind which he stood in battle. It was an overall defense against attack because he could turn it in every direction to stop the arrows aimed at him. *In addition to all this, take up the shield of faith, with which you can extinguish all the flaming arrows of the evil one (Ephesians 6:16).*

When you and I look at our circumstances, at times we can get discouraged. However, when we protect ourselves with our shield of faith and believe that God's Word is true regardless of our circumstances, we can come through victoriously.

The fiery arrows of the enemy may include arrows of doubt, depression, condemnation, fear or confusion. The list goes on and on. We need to keep up our spiritual shields, so that when the enemy shoots arrows our way, we can respond with faith. Remember, "Faith comes by hearing, and hearing by the word of God" (Romans 10:17). Let's speak forth the promises of the Word of God and not allow the fiery arrows of the evil one to begin to burn a hole in our spiritual armor. We need to quickly extinguish them by speaking and believing the Word of God.

Even though we live in an instant society, we need to learn to live by faith. We may not always get results immediately, but we should continue to believe God's Word as truth, even in the midst of seemingly insurmountable circumstances. God is faithful. We can trust Him as we keep our shield of faith held high.

REFLECTION

How do we defend ourselves from Satan's "flaming arrows"?

A few years ago, I met a lady whose son had strayed from the faith. While he was in rebellion, she continued to believe God would speak to him. She knew the Lord had given her a promise in Isaiah 59:21b...*My words that I have put in your mouth will not depart from your mouth, or from the mouths of your children....* This mother chose to believe God's Word. As she kept her shield of faith high, her son was convicted by the Lord at an unlikely place—a rock and roll concert! Today he is a pastor. Remember, we live by faith and not by sight!

Your helmet and sword

Much of the Christian's battle is in the mind. Neither a Christian or a soldier fighting a battle would fight very well if he did not have the hope of victory. We need to protect our heads with the helmet of salvation because the hope of salvation will defend our soul and keep it from the blows of the enemy. The helmet of salvation gives us the hope of continual safety and protection, built on the promises of God. *Take the helmet of salvation...(Ephesians 6:17a).*

Remember, to be *saved* does not only mean *to be set free from sin and live eternally with God.* Salvation also includes *healing, deliverance* and *to be set free from the powers of darkness.* I often travel to nations that do not have the same quality of medical expertise that we have in our western culture. I am amazed at the ability of God's people to truly believe Him for everyday miracles in these settings. It is impossible to figure out how miracles work. We simply accept by faith that God is a God of miracles. Our helmet of salvation keeps us from being confused by the powers of darkness and helps us to rely on God's great salvation and healing.

The Lord tells us to take up the final piece of armor—the sword of the Spirit. The sword was the only piece of armor a soldier carried that was offensive as well as defensive. For a Christian, the sword of the Spirit is the powerful Word of God...*and the sword of the Spirit, which is the word of God. And pray in the Spirit on all occasions with all kinds of prayers and requests. With this in mind, be alert and always keep on praying for all the saints (Ephesians 6:17b-18).*

When we are armed with the truth of God's Word, the Holy Spirit living within us helps us deal with temptations that come our way. We do not rely on our own wisdom, but on the Lord's. When we know His Word, we can withstand Satan's lies. As we hide the Word of God in our hearts (Psalms 119:11), we can resist sin.

The Bible tells us that the gates of hell will not prevail against the church of Jesus Christ. As Christians, we are called to take over enemy territory. Do not settle for less. Take the Word of God seriously and confess it, believe it, live it, and expect to experience it in your life.

In order to be alert and stand our ground, the Bible says (Ephesians 6:13) that we must take up the whole armor of God. We must put on the belt of truth and the breastplate of righteousness. We prepare ourselves with the gospel of peace and take up the shield of faith. In addition, we use the helmet of salvation and the sword of the Spirit. All this armor is a protection and helps us to pray effectively. Paul, the apostle, says we should pray always and be watchful as we pray for all the saints. We are called to pray for one another. Spiritual warfare calls for intensity of prayer. It is not an option, it is a life and death matter.

REFLECTION
How does the helmet of salvation help us fight the battle? Why is the sword of the Spirit so important?

Ready for action!

We really do need to pray for one another. Prayer allows us to enter the conflict of spiritual warfare and win the victory by working with God in this way. Paul, the apostle, asks for prayer in Ephesians 6:19-20 so he could be bold in his witness for Christ. *Pray also for me, that whenever I open my mouth, words may be given me so that I will fearlessly make known the mystery of the gospel, for which I am an ambassador in chains. Pray that I may declare it fearlessly, as I should.*

The Lord wants us to be bold witnesses for Jesus Christ, but boldness comes from our prayer closet. As we pray for those in our small groups, churches, youth groups, communities, homes and workplaces, we will experience the boldness of the Lord to proclaim His Word to our generation. One time, while I was in the nation of Scotland, I found myself compelled to speak to a young man that I met on the street about Jesus. I knew that my boldness to speak out came because of prayer warriors who were praying for me.

If Paul, the apostle, needed others to pray for him to be bold, how much more do we need to be praying for one another to be bold today? In order for us to fulfill the Great Commission, we must be people of prayer. Remember to pray for missionaries the Lord has placed in your life to be bold for the Lord. And as we put on the full armor of God and pray each day, we will listen to our heavenly Father for orders from heaven. Then we will experience Jesus using us to make disciples in our generation.

It has been my experience that most spiritual failure happens when Christians fail to keep their spiritual armor in place. When you get up in the morning, declare that your armor is in place. Declare that you have placed the belt of truth around your waist. You are righteous through faith in Jesus Christ; the breastplate is in place. You have peace with God through your Lord Jesus Christ (Romans 5:1) because you are justified through faith. You walk in complete forgiveness toward anyone who's hurt you and you have pursued peace with them as much as possible (Romans 12:18). You have taken up the shield of faith and will not allow the fiery darts of the enemy to hurt you. You will quench them in Jesus' name through faith in the Word of God. The helmet of salvation is secure. You know you are born again and that Jesus Christ has changed your life. You take the Word of God and boldly, aggres-

REFLECTION

When we pour our lives out for others, what are we promised in Luke 6:38? In Proverbs 11:25?

sively confront the powers of darkness in Jesus' name. You pray as a soldier who has properly placed on the armor that the Lord Jesus has given. You are ready for action! The world around us is waiting for us to declare the truth that will set them free.

CHAPTER 3

Reaching the Lost and Making Disciples

KEY MEMORY VERSE

"Come, follow me," Jesus said, "and I will make you fishers of men."
Mark 1:17

True evangelism

God places a much higher priority on evangelism than we usually do. Why? Because God truly loves people. *"God so loved the world..." (John 3:16).* As Christians, we often become ingrown and look within instead of trying to find ways to help people around us. God has called us to look outward. God's heart is for the world—for people. Evangelism is sharing the good news of Jesus Christ with others.

Many times Christians have a warped understanding of what evangelism really is. Some think that evangelism means they must knock on doors and pass out gospel tracts. Although this can be an effective way to share your faith, the Lord may not call you to evangelize in that way. To others, evangelism means going to crusades. Praise God for crusades, but for most Christians, crusade evangelism is not the type of evangelism they are called to.

I believe evangelism for most people is being so filled with Jesus that wherever they go, they discover people who need a relationship with God. Our responsibility is to share with people what God has done in our lives and help to encourage them to receive the good news of Jesus Christ into their lives.

REFLECTION
What does evangelism mean to you? How did Jesus evangelize?

In the story of the Good Samaritan (Luke 10:33-37), the Samaritan found a man lying in the gutter and helped him even though some of the religious folks of his day passed on by without lending a hand. The Samaritan practiced the principles of the kingdom of God by loving the person whom God brought into his path. Jesus made it very clear that we should *love the Lord...and love your neighbor as yourself (Luke 10:27).*

Loving God is a call to love others. Compassion for the lost and those in need is a sign that we really love God. After Jesus told the story of the Good Samaritan, he quizzed a nearby religious leader, *"Who was a neighbor to the man who fell into the hands of robbers?" The expert in the law replied, "The one who had mercy on him." Jesus told him, "Go and do likewise" (Luke 10:37).*

We must operate in mercy and love. In Luke 15, Jesus gave three more stories about loving those around us. The first story was the parable of the lost sheep. Out of 100 sheep, one got lost, and the shepherd searched until he found it. The second parable involved a lost coin. The owner of the coin looked all day for it, putting all his effort into finding it. The third story is that of a prodigal son who took half of his father's fortune and left home to do his own thing. The Bible tells us his father waited for him and then reached out lovingly when his son returned.

You see, God places a high priority on people who are hurting or lost. God has called us to reach out to those around us, even the "unlovely," so He can fulfill His purposes through us. Jesus has called us to be fishers of men. *"Come, follow me," Jesus said, "and I will make you fishers of men" (Mark 1:17).*

Let's learn together how we can "catch men" and lead them to faith in Jesus Christ.

The *oikos* principle

DAY 2

How did Jesus and the early church lead people to faith? We sometimes call this the *"oikos* principle." The Greek word *oikos* means *household* or *family.* Our *oikos* includes those with whom we relate on a regular basis. O*ikos* refers to one's personal community or those with whom we are in relationship.

The scriptures tell us in Acts 10 that there was a man named Cornelius—a devout man who feared God with all his household, gave generously to the poor, and prayed to God regularly. One day Cornelius received a supernatural visitation from God through a vision. God told him to send messengers and call for Peter who would give him a message from God. Peter came to meet Cornelius who was...*expecting them and had called together his relatives and close friends (Acts 10:24).* Cornelius invited his *oikos* (relatives and friends) to this meeting with Peter and many of those people came to know Jesus Christ.

Another story showing how God used someone's oikos to bring people to Jesus occurs in Acts 16. Paul and Silas were in prison when an earthquake opened all the doors. The jailer was going to kill himself because he thought the prisoners would escape and he would be held responsible. Paul told him to refrain from harming himself because all the prisoners were safe. When Paul shared the Word of God with the jailer, his entire *oikos* (household) came to know Jesus Christ. All of us have people in our lives who are placed there by the Lord. They are the people with whom we can share the gospel most effectively and easily. No matter where we live in the world, the *oikos* strategy or building by relationship is the most natural way of fulfilling the Great Commission. People want the truth. They are waiting for Christians whom they can trust to give them the truth.

You may want to list your *oikos* members on a sheet of paper. Pray and ask God to show you two or three of the people whom you're most concerned about and begin to pray for these people and reach out to them. If they are unsaved, you will be involved in evangelism. If they are struggling in their Christian lives, God may call you to be involved in discipleship by becoming a spiritual father or mother to them.

The scriptures tell us in the book of Acts that new believers were *added* to the church daily as they were being saved (Acts 2:47). However, as we continue to read the book of Acts, we see the Lord taking the church another step. God's people began to grow in numbers. *Then the churches throughout all Judea, Galilee, and Samaria had peace and were edified.*

And walking in the fear of the Lord and in the comfort of the Holy Spirit, they were multiplied (Acts 9:31 NKJ).

REFLECTION
What does "oikos" mean? List people in your oikos.

God's will is for us to be *multiplying* ourselves. In order for us to multiply, we need to get our eyes off ourselves and reach out to those who need to experience the life and power of Jesus Christ. We will see God's kingdom expand and our own spiritual growth accelerate. Jesus spent His time here on this earth doing two things—talking to God about people and talking to people about God. He has called us to do the same.

Kinds of people in your *oikos*

There are several groups of people in our *oikos* or personal community. First of all, there are family members and relatives. Your uncle Jack and aunt Sally are all part of your *oikos*, even if they live far away. If you maintain regular contact with them, they are part of your *oikos*. Second, those who share common interests with you are part of your *oikos*. They may play sports with you or share an interest in computers, or sewing...the list goes on. Third, those who live in your geographical location are part of your *oikos*—this, of course, includes your neighbors.

Those with whom you share a common vocation—your fellow employees—would fit into a fourth category. The fifth area of persons that are part of your *oikos* would be others with whom you have regular contact, including your dentist, family doctor, auto mechanic, sales people, school officials, classmates, and so on. People in your *oikos* group will be much more receptive to the gospel because they trust you—you have built a relationship with them.

When Levi invited Jesus for dinner, he invited his *oikos* members or business associates. Luke 5:29 tells us of this occasion, *Then Levi held a great banquet for Jesus at his house, and a large crowd of tax collectors and others were eating with them.*

Because Levi already had a relationship with them, these tax collectors gladly came to listen to what Jesus had to say. Jesus had the opportunity to share with members of Levi's *oikos,* and they were presented with the hope Jesus offered. When we invite our *oikos* to meet Jesus, they have the opportunity to be presented with the truth that will set them free.

Nathanael was Philip's *oikos* member; they lived in the same town. Through their friendship, Philip led Nathanael to faith in Jesus Christ. The Bible tells us in John 1:45 that...*Philip found Nathanael and told him, "We have found the one Moses wrote about in the Law, and about whom the prophets also wrote—Jesus of Nazareth..."*

The scriptures are filled with examples of people who came to know Jesus through someone with whom they had a relationship. Sometime back, a small group leader in our church received a phone call from a woman in his small group. "Do you have any holy water?" he

REFLECTION
Explain how you have released your faith in the past week.

was asked. The group leader did not grow up in a Roman Catholic tradition and was not expecting this type of request. When he asked her for further details, she shared her concern for her daughter and her daughter's boyfriend. Strange things were happening in their home. An object had jumped off the stove and other unexplainable supernatural things were happening in their house. "May I come over to your daughter and her boyfriend's home to pray?" he asked.

"Oh yes," she explained, "and I want to be there when you come." The small group leader and his wife went over to the young couple's home to pray. After a time of sharing the Word of God, the young man received Jesus Christ as Lord. His girlfriend also expressed a desire to follow the Lord, and they were married a short time later. The demonic occurrences in their home stopped when the couple was set free spiritually. It all happened through a small group *oikos* relationship that expanded to include family *oikos* relationships. *Oikos* evangelism has a way of multiplying outward!

Spend time mentoring others

Jesus Christ called us to make disciples. The key to making disciples can be found in Mark 3:14-15a. *He appointed twelve...that they might be with him and that he might send them out to preach and to have authority....*

Jesus was looking for twelve men with whom He could spend time so that He could show them the principles of the kingdom of God. He wanted His disciples to experience God's principles as He modeled these truths for them through His own life. Discipleship often involves this kind of training through mentoring or modeling.

Jesus reached out to the disciples for companionship and training, so that they might, in turn, go out to minister themselves. Dicipling others is caring for them as friends and training them to grow in their Christian lives. Making disciples is not telling other people what to do. Making disciples is literally laying down our lives for others and taking the time needed to see them grow spiritually. We can pray, encourage and help others focus on the Word of God which gives clear instructions how we should live our lives in Christ.

REFLECTION
List some practical ways we can make ourselves available to train disciples.

Biblical discipleship reminds me of serving as a coach for a sports team. The coach's responsibility is to help his players to be the best they can possibly be. Unless we are reaching out and helping others, we become stagnant and ingrown. Like an ingrown toenail, pain will eventually occur. God has called us to reach out to others and train them at the same time.

The Dead Sea is world-renowned "stagnant" sea. Waters run into it, but nothing runs out. There is life in a river, but a sense of death remains in a stagnant pool. When we give out to others, the power and life of God will flow freely through our lives.

Learn and teach by example

I love to play the guitar. I have had the privilege of teaching many others to play the guitar during the past 25 years. In fact, many of my students now play the guitar much better than I. If I taught you how to play the guitar, I would sit down with you and a guitar. I'd show you how to play by teaching you exactly where to hold your fingers on the frets and how to hold the pick as you began to strum.

The same principle applies to the kingdom of God. We are called to train, love and show others how to become disciples of Jesus Christ. You may say, "Larry, I have only been a Christian for less than a year." Great! You can begin to show others what you have learned in the past year. God wants us to immediately reach out to those around us and help them come into the kingdom. The good news is that we don't have to know all the answers. God is the One who has the answers. We can freely share with others that we don't have all the answers, but our God does. In fact, the Bible tells us in Deuteronomy 29:29, *The secret things belong to the Lord our God, but the things revealed belong to us and to our children forever, that we may follow all the words of this law.*

The Bible makes it clear that we are responsible to act on those things that have been revealed to us by the Lord. Even when we don't have the answers to some of life's problems, the Lord will bring into our lives spiritual fathers or mothers who will be used by the Holy Spirit to help and guide us. Then the Lord will help us to do the same—to serve others and be a spiritual father or mother to them. As we work together, we can see God's kingdom built as dozens and hundreds of lives in our communities are changed through the power of Jesus Christ.

Imagine, for a moment, every Christian you know, training two or three others in the basic truths and experiences of walking with Jesus. These "disciples" would be encouraged to do the same. The results would be astounding. In fact, if you and I each discipled another believer every six months and encouraged each person we disciple to do the same, and the pattern was repeated every six months, in less than 30 years the entire population of the world could be won to Christ!

REFLECTION
What are we responsible for, according to Deuteronomy 29:29? How can we pass on what we have learned to others?

Hospitality in homes

Do you know that one of the most powerful ways we can be involved in discipleship and evangelism is through hospitality? Hospitality is a biblical principle that simply means *cheerfully sharing food and shelter and spiritual refreshment with those that God brings into our lives.* 1 Peter 4:9 tells us, *Offer hospitality to one another without grumbling.*

I believe the Lord wants to use our homes to build His church. Our homes are to be used as places where people can be encouraged, filled with the Holy Spirit and come to know Jesus Christ. The presence of God is in your home because Jesus Christ lives in you.

Because Christ lives in you, you can be assured that every place you go, the presence of God will be there—in your home, at school, at the local restaurant, or at the store. God's kingdom can be built as we eat breakfast with another person, laugh together, cry together, or just have fun sharing life together. The principle of hospitality can be a tremendous blessing as we make disciples and fulfill the Great Commission.

The book of Acts opens and closes in a home. Homes are so important to the work of the kingdom of God. Dr. Cho, the pastor of the largest church in the world located in Seoul, Korea, was asked the question, "Where is God's address?" His answer was that

REFLECTION
What does hospitality mean to you? How should we offer hospitality, according to 1 Peter 4:9?

God's address is *our* address. In other words, God lives inside you and me. Wherever you live, wherever you are, that is where God is. There are many people who would not feel free to go to a church meeting, but they would talk to you while sitting in your house eating a meal or playing a game in your living-room.

Romans 12:13 tells us that we should "practice hospitality." You may think, "My home is not nice enough to invite people in." Be assured, when people come into your home, they will sense the presence of God because He lives in you—they won't care about your house. When my wife, LaVerne, and I were first married, much of our hospitality was in a tiny mobile home. We had people coming in and staying overnight, eating with us and praying with us, and they did not care that it was small. Expect the Lord to use your home, no matter what size, to build His kingdom.

Sowing spiritual seeds in others' lives

Praying, reaching the lost and making disciples is a bit like sowing seed in a garden. When we sow spiritual seeds into people's lives through prayer, encouragement and discipleship, we expect to get a crop eventually. We sow that seed in faith.

If I go out to my garden and dig up the seed every day and say, "I don't think it's growing," I will never get a crop. In the same way, we sow the truth of God's Word into people's lives in faith, knowing that regardless of what we see today, we will get a crop in due time. We know, because we sowed our seeds in faith.

The scriptures tell us in Mark 4, that when we sow the seed of the Word of God into people's lives, several things can happen. For one, individuals may hear God's Word but fail to respond to it because Satan immediately steals it away (v. 15). It is at these times that we should bind demonic bondages in seekers' lives, so they can be free to hear and accept God's Word.

The scriptures also tell us that some people will hear the Word of God and immediately receive it with gladness. However, their roots are shallow, and they only endure for a time. When they go through hard times, they immediately stumble (v. 16).

Others may hear the Word but allow the things of this world to get in the way of their commitment to Christ. *Still others, like seed sown among thorns, hear the word; but the worries of this life, the deceitfulness of wealth and the desires for other things come in and choke the word, making it unfruitful (Mark 4:18-19).* Because of the worries of this life, these people may find the Word of God being choked from their lives. If we sow seeds of encouragement into their lives and pray for them, we can keep the spiritual thorns from choking the Word of God out of their lives. They need some extra assistance during this time. Do you know that some varieties of trees, when first planted, need to have a stake driven into the ground next to the tree? A rope then is tied around the tree and stake until the tree can grow tall and strong enough to hold itself. God has called you and me to be "stakes" for people, helping to stabilize their lives until they can make it on their own.

Finally there are those who hear God's Word and believe and persevere. They will bear fruit according to Mark 4:20. *Others, like seed sown on good soil, hear the word, accept it, and produce a crop—thirty, sixty or even a hundred times what was sown.*

As the Spirit of God, through us, pours His Word into people's lives, we are going to see a mighty harvest of people coming to know Jesus Christ. Someday we are going to stand before the Lord accompanied by multitudes of others—they are the result of the seeds that were sown—multiplying in numbers by the grace of God.

Have you ever heard of Mordecai Ham? Very few people have heard of him, and yet he has had a profound effect on the nations of the world. While Mordecai was preaching at a revival meeting in a tent, a young man came one evening and gave his life to Jesus. That man's name was Billy Graham. Every person who has come to know Jesus Christ through Billy Graham's ministry is a product of the obedience of a man named Mordecai Ham.

D. L. Moody, a hundred years ago, was responsible for leading more than a million people to Jesus Christ. Yet the man who shared the gospel with Mr. Moody was a common, ordinary man who made a decision to share Christ with the young boys in his Sunday School class. The Bible says the mustard seed is the smallest of all seeds, but grows to be a majestic tree (Matthew 13:31-32). As we are obedient to God in the "little areas," the Lord promises there will be a great spiritual harvest.

The Great Commission is simply sowing seed. Good spiritual seed is sown through prayer, encouragement, and by sharing the Word of God with others. As we continue to sow in obedience, the seed will grow. The multiplication process will continue on and

REFLECTION
How do you sow spiritual seeds? What does faith have to do with planting seeds in others' lives?

on. Healthy Christians are those who pray and reach out to those whom God brings into their lives. Let's rise up in faith together and labor with Jesus to fulfill the Great Commission.

CHAPTER 4

You Are Called to Be a Spiritual Father or Mother!

The need for spiritual fathers and mothers

Jesus invested three years of His earthly ministry in the lives of twelve men. It was valuable time spent fathering His spiritual children. This time of mentoring prepared and equipped the disciples to "go into all the world" and fulfill the Great Commission.

We briefly mentioned the concept of "spiritual fathering and mothering" earlier in this book. While "discipleship" is similar in that it involves a few people getting together and helping the younger Christian, spiritual parenting has a much wider scope. Spiritual parenting has the intention of developing and encouraging others to walk the path of becoming spiritual fathers and mothers themselves. The spiritual father or mother mentors and trains another, and in doing so, imparts his or her inheritance to the younger Christian.

New Christians desperately need spiritual fathers or mothers to nurture and encourage them in their spiritual walk. The man who served as a pastor in my church for many years told me that when he received Christ, he was in his mid-twenties. A 77-year-old "spiritual father" from his church took him under his wing and discipled him. It made all the difference for this future pastor's spiritual maturity.

Paul, the apostle, told the Corinthian church that they should not overlook the need to make lasting spiritual investments in others' lives. He said they had many guardians or teachers in the church, but not many spiritual fathers and mothers who were willing to spend time nurturing new believers, according to 1 Corinthians 4:14-15. *I am not writing this to shame you, but to warn you, as my dear children. Even though you have ten thousand guardians in Christ, you do not have many fathers....*

These Christians were immature as believers because they lacked true fathers to give them an identity and proper training and nurturing. They needed spiritual fathers and mothers who were willing to spend time with them.

Many times, new believers

REFLECTION
Why were the Christians immature in 1 Corinthians 4:14-15 Do you sense a need for a spiritua father or mother to equip you to "go into the world"?
Are you willing to become a spiritual father or mother?

never really grow to their full potential in God because they never had a spiritual parent to care for them. True spiritual parents are sincerely concerned about the welfare of their spiritual children.

God wants to "turn the hearts of the fathers to the children"

Why is raising up spiritual parents who are willing to nurture spiritual children and help them grow up in their Christian lives so important? For one, it is a fulfillment of the Lord's promise in the last days to...*turn the hearts of the fathers to the children, and the hearts of the children to their fathers...(Malachi 4:6).*

The Lord wants to restore harmony among fathers and their children, both naturally and spiritually, so fathers can freely impart their inheritance to the next generation. He wants spiritual fathers and mothers to take up the mantle to train their children so they no longer flounder in the sea of life. Children need to have the kind of parents in their lives providing the character they need, telling them they are valuable, that they are gifts from God. Parents need to put expectation into children's hearts so that they believe in themselves.

Paul says in verse 17 of 1 Corinthians 4 that he is going to send Timothy to the Corinthian church because he would *remind you of my way of life in Christ Jesus.* As a spiritual father, Paul faithfully trained Timothy. Now Timothy was ready to impart *his* spiritual fatherhood to the Corinthian church. Christian believers need to see spiritual fathering and mothering modeled so they can be equipped to pass on a legacy to the next generation of believers.

Paul trained Timothy, his beloved and trustworthy spiritual son, and now Timothy was coming to train them. Paul trusted Timothy to help the Corinthian church because Paul had trained him like a son. With this example, they would soon be producing their own spiritual sons and daughters. This kind of mentoring relationship of training and equipping sons and daughters was a spiritual investment that could continue to multiply as equipped and mature believers went out into the world to spread the gospel.

REFLECTION
Why is it important for spiritual parents to take up the mantle and train their children? What happens when spiritual sons and daughters are mentored and equipped by spiritual parents?

Spiritual children go through growth stages

According to the Bible, we go through life in stages—as little children, young men, and fathers. At each point in our journey, we function in a particular way and have distinct tasks to perform. John addresses all three spiritual stages in *1 John 2:12-14. I write to you, little children, because your sins are forgiven you for His name's sake. I write to you, fathers, because you have known Him who is from the beginning. I write to you, young men, because you have overcome the wicked one. I write to you, little children, because you have known the Father. I have written to you, fathers, because you have known Him who is from the beginning. I have written to you, young men, because you are strong, and the word of God abides in you, and you have overcome the wicked one.*

Coming to a place of fatherhood is the cry of God's heart. Since fatherhood is so crucial to God's divine order, He established a natural training ground consisting of "growth stages." Baby Christians grow to fatherhood as they progress through each of these stages. Only then can they receive the heart and revelation of a father or mother.

Our stages as babies in Christ, young men and women, and spiritual fathers and mothers have nothing to do with our chronological age but everything to do with how we eventually progress on to spiritual maturity. Children are expected to grow up. Only then can they become fathers and mothers.

If we fail to take the next steps to become spiritual parents, we remain spiritual babies—spiritually immature and lacking parenting skills. It is sad, but it is this scenario which is often the very case in the church. Many times there is no provision for believers to develop within our church systems.

Nevertheless, with the restoration of New Testament Christianity, as people meet together in small groups, God is providing an ideal setting to develop spiritual parents. Each person is given the opportunity to "do the work of ministry" and connect in vital relationships with each other. Through modeling and impartation, spiritual reproduction happens naturally.

God's intention is to bring new believers to the place of spiritual fatherhood and motherhood after going through spiritual childhood and young adulthood. Paul, the apostle made it his concern to properly instruct everyone so they could be grounded in the faith...*teaching every man in all wisdom, that we may present every man perfect in Christ Jesus (Colossians 1:28).*

The Lord's call has not changed. Every believer, after being equipped, can become a spiritual parent. Meanwhile, we have to progress through the stages of growth. Let's look at each of these three stages in Days 4-5.

REFLECTION
What are the growth stages for a new Christian to become a spiritual parent himself? What happens if we fail to go through these stages?

Growing from spiritual children to young men and women

Spiritual babies in the body of Christ are wonderful! According to 1 John 2:12, they are *"children whose sins are forgiven."* This forgiveness of sin puts them in fellowship with God and other believers. Spiritual children or new believers are alive to what they can receive from their Savior. They freely ask the Father when they have a need. Did you ever notice how new believers can pray prayers that seem to be theologically unsound, yet God answers almost every prayer a new believer prays? The Father is quick to take care of these little ones.

A new believer's focus is forgiveness of sins, getting to heaven and getting to know the Father. Like natural babies, they know their Father, although it is not necessarily a thorough knowledge of God. A new believer will often act like a natural child with the marks of immaturity, including instability and gullibility. They will need constant assurance and care. They often do the unexpected because they are still learning what it means to follow Jesus. Spiritual parents are happy to spend extra time with spiritual children in order to guide them in the right direction.

But what happens when spiritual babies do not grow up? Not only new believers are spiritual babies in the church today. Older Christians who lack spiritual maturity are "adults in age" but "babies in spiritual growth." They may be 20, 30, 40 or 50 years of age, Christian believers for years, and have never spiritually matured. They live self-centered life-styles, complaining and fussing and throwing temper-tantrums when things do not go their way. Some do not accept the fact that God loves them for who they are.

Others may wallow in self-pity when they fail. Many spiritual children in our churches today desperately need to grow up and move on to the next stage as spiritual young men and women.

Spiritual young men and women no longer have to be spoon-fed. According to 1 John 2:14, *the Word of God abides in them and they have learned to feed on the Word to overcome the wicked one.* They don't need to run to others in the church to care for them like babies because they have learned how to apply the Word to their own lives. When the devil tempts them, they know what to do to overcome him. They use God's Word effectively and powerfully!

Spiritual young men and women must be encouraged (1 Timothy 4:12). They are strong in the Word and Spirit. They have learned to use the strength of spiritual discipline, of prayer and the study of the Word. They are alive to what they can do for Jesus.

On the other hand, the temptations of spiritual youth may be a trap for those who have not yet developed a strong sense of right and wrong. Youth are cautioned to run from their youthful passions that might lead to scandal (2 Timothy 2:22).

Spiritual young men or women may have attained a certain level of spiritual maturity, but they are not yet spiritual parents. They sometimes can become arrogant and dogmatic. After returning from the latest seminar or after reading a recent book, they may think they have all of the answers. They need to be tempered by parenthood. They must become fathers and mothers to experience its joys and disciplines. Again, it bears repeating: becoming a spiritual parent has nothing to do with chronological age; it is a spiritual age!

REFLECTION
What are some characteristics of spiritual children? Of spiritual young men and women?

Spiritual fathers and mothers defined

DAY 5

Just how do spiritual young men and women grow up to become spiritual fathers and mothers? There is only one way—to have children! You can become a spiritual parent either by natural birth (fathering someone you have personally led to Christ) or by adoption (fathering someone who is already a believer but needs to be mentored). Paul led Onesimus to Christ personally, so Onesimus was his natural spiritual son (Philemon 10). Timothy was also Paul's spiritual son, but by spiritual "adoption" because Timothy came to Christ earlier through the influence of his mother and grandmother (Acts 16).

Spiritual fathers and mothers are mature believers who have grown and matured in their Christian walk; they are called *fathers* according to 1 John 2:13. *I write to you, fathers, because you have known Him who is from the beginning....* This implies a profound and thorough knowledge of Jesus through knowing His Word. It also implies a deep sense of acquaintance with Him, by having a passion for Jesus.

Mature Christians are awake to their calling to be like Jesus—to be a father like God's Son. They understand what it takes to be a spiritual parent and are willing to become one.

REFLECTION
How do spiritual young men and women become parents? Give a definition of a spiritual father or mother.

One of the greatest catalysts to maturity as a Christian is to become a spiritual parent. Even if prospective spiritual parents do not feel ready to become parents, as they take a step of faith, and draw on the help and advice of their own spiritual mom and dad, they will find great success and fulfillment.

Spiritual fathers and mothers could be called *mentors* or *coaches* because they are in a place to help sons and daughters negotiate the obstacles of their spiritual journeys. A coach is someone who wants to see you win. A coach tells you that you can make it.

Simply stated, my favorite definition of a spiritual father or mother is: ***A spiritual father or mother helps a spiritual son or daughter reach his or her God-given potential.***

With a mature spiritual parent at their side, sons and daughters will grow strong and learn quickly and naturally by example. The parent teaches, trains, sets a good example, and provides a role model. Spiritual parents raise children's awareness of attitudes or behaviors in their lives that need to be changed. They help new believers take an honest look at their lives and make adjustments so that their actions and behaviors can change.

Our inheritance of spiritual children

Regardless of our own experience—whether or not we have had a spiritual father or mother—we can become a spiritual father or mother to someone the Lord has placed in our lives. Every believer can make a decision to co-labor with Jesus and make disciples by becoming a spiritual father or mother to someone who needs our assistance to grow in the Lord.

So how do we begin? The early Christians did not haphazardly "share their faith." Instead, people were built together, each doing a job, working as a team to accomplish the Great Commission. God will place people in our lives He wants us to reach out to. As we commit ourselves to train them, they will become conformed to Jesus' likeness. As new believers grow in Christ, they also will begin to make disciples, following the parent's example. Abraham was ninety-nine years old when God gave him the promise that he would be the *father of many nations (Genesis 17:4).* Galatians 3:29 says that those who belong to Christ are *Abraham's seed, and heirs according to the promise.* Therefore, as believers, God wants to birth in us "nations," too. These "nations" or groups of people, who come to know God because of our influence, will be our spiritual lineage—they are our posterity in God's kingdom. We have been promised it because we are children of promise. Our God desires to give us a spiritual posterity.

Years ago, I was a spiritual father to Bill, now a missionary in the Caribbean. On a visit to Barbados, Bill told me an interesting history of this island nation. Many of the people who now live in Barbados originally

REFLECTION
How can we birth a spiritual lineage according to Galatians 3:29?

came as slaves from West Africa, specifically the nation of Gambia. Today, native Barbadians are being sent out from Barbados as missionaries to Gambia. Then he said something that moved me deeply, "Larry, do you realize the people being reached in Gambia are part of your spiritual heritage? You were one of my spiritual fathers." At the time I was a spiritual father to Bill, I was a young man myself, a chicken farmer, who led a Bible study of young people. Bill had gone into the world and trained others to go, and the results mushroomed! I was deeply moved! It was as if I was the recipient of a large inheritance!

Go into all the world and leave a legacy!

The promise of spiritual children is for every Christian! God has placed us here on earth because He has called us to become spiritual fathers and mothers in our generation. With this comes the expectation that our spiritual children will have more spiritual children and continue into infinity.

Our inheritance will be all the spiritual children that we can some day present to Jesus Christ. *For what is our hope, our joy, or the crown in which we will glory in the presence of our Lord Jesus when he comes? Is it not you? Indeed, you are our glory and joy (1 Thessalonians 2:19-20).* No matter what you do—whether you are a housewife, a student, a worker in a factory, a pastor of a church, or the head a large corporation—you have the divine blessing and responsibility to birth spiritual children, grandchildren and great grandchildren. You are called to impart to others the rich inheritance that God has promised.

If we would get serious about making disciples one at a time and training them so they could go and make more disciples, it would not take long for every person on the face of the earth to be confronted with the truth of Jesus Christ. This scriptural principle is so simple, yet many times God's people have failed to obey this Great Commission from our Lord Jesus. God has called us and given us His priority to make disciples.

God uses the principle of multiplication through spiritual fathering and mothering. When you and I are obedient to Him, reaching out to one, two, three, four or more people whom the Lord places in our lives, we will literally see God's kingdom being established over the whole world. God wants to establish His kingdom in our generation through the principle of multiplication through spiritual parenting. God's kingdom is built as we love people and spend time with them.

If you desire more training to become a spiritual father or mother, you may want to read my book, *The Cry for Spiritual Fathers and Mothers.* There is also a video training available.[1] Now that you have learned the basic foundations of the Christian life through this *Biblical Foundation Series*, pray about helping someone else grow in the Lord and teach them what you have learned!

I believe an end-time sweeping revival is just around the corner. God's people need to be alert and ready to accommodate the great harvest this will bring into the kingdom of God. Spiritual parents must be ready to obey His call and take young Christians under their wings.

We are containers of the Holy Spirit, and God is going to pour His Spirit out on us that flows to others. Acts 2:17 tells us, *"In the last days,"* God says, *"I will pour out my Spirit on all people. Your sons and daughters will prophesy, your young men will see visions, your old men will dream dreams."*

REFLECTION

What is our spiritual legacy? How does having and becoming a spiritual parent help you obey the Great Commission?

Someday, you and I will stand before the Living God. When I stand before the Lord, I do not want to stand there by myself. How about you? Let's stand there with a multitude of our spiritual children, grandchildren and their future descendants! The Lord wants to give you a spiritual legacy. God has called you to be a spiritual parent!

[1] Larry Kreider, *The Cry for Spiritual Fathers and Mothers*, (Ephrata, PA: House to House Publications, 2000). See page 64 for ordering information.

Daily Devotional Extra Days

If you are using this book as a daily devotional, you will notice there are 28 days in this study. Depending on the month, you may need the three extra days' studies given here.

Obeying the Great Commission

Read John 17:13-18. How will we have Christ's joy fulfilled in us? What has Jesus been praying for us? How can we be set apart unto God? Has this book changed the way you are living in order to obey the Great Commission?

Making Disciples

Read 1 Peter 2:21-24. What are some areas of life in which we need to imitate our Lord Jesus? How did Jesus respond to adverse situations? What can we learn from this passage about true discipleship? Are you reaching out, discipling and allowing God to work through you to multiply His kingdom?

Go Find a Son (or Daughter)

Read 1 Kings 19. What solution does God give a discouraged and depressed Elijah (v.19)? What happened when Elijah obeyed? Elijah's spiritual son Elisha experienced a double portion of the Lord's Spirit. Should we expect our spiritual children to progress far beyond us spiritually?

What is the Great Commission?

1. Go and make disciples
   a. Jesus' last minute instructions for His disciples. Matthew 28:18-20
   b. A commission is a set of instructions. *Going* is not an option with Jesus' instructions to make disciples of the nations.
   c. Everywhere we go, we are called to make disciples.

2. Reach the nations
   a. Christians are commanded to reach people of all nations. Matthew 28:19
   b. Missionaries are those who hear the call to live out their witness for Jesus in another country.
   c. Missionaries want to see the gospel penetrate the hearts of people in the societies in which they live.
   d. Every believer should be involved in world missions in some way.

3. The strategy
   a. The Great Commission is a call to make disciples, and we can start right where we live.
   b. Disciples are made one at a time. Jesus ministered to multitudes but spent most of His time with the twelve disciples, training them.
   c. The church is built through relationships (1 Peter 2:5). How can you make disciples within your various spheres of friendships?
   d. God's intention is use us to raise up spiritual parents who train spiritual children (younger Christians) to come to maturity.

4. **Relationships last forever**
   a. The early church experienced family-type relationships as they met together in homes to nurture, equip and serve each other (Acts 2:46-47).
   b. Ask God to show you those relationships you should "pour your life into."
   c. The gospel is powerful (Romans 1:16; 1 Corinthians 1:18) and will explode in people's lives because of our influence.
      Ex: Welsh revival in early 1900's

5. **Your life is read like a book**
   a. Paul told the early Christians to imitate him.
      1 Corinthians 11:1
   b. The only spiritual book that some ever read is the book of our lives (2 Corinthians 3:2-3).

6. **Minor on differences; major on Jesus**
   a. We must focus on Jesus (Matthew 6:33) and making disciples and not be distracted by problems and difference in the church (Romans 14:5).
   b. Jesus wants us to be unified (John 17:20-21).
   c. Christ is coming back for a spotless bride (Ephesians 5:27).

7. **Prayer, evangelism and discipleship**
   a. A three-legged stool of truth: God uses prayer, evangelism and discipleship to build His church.
   b. Giving our lives to help others by praying for them, reaching out to them and discipling them is a blessing.
   c. We will be blessed in return (Luke 6:38; Ecclesiastes 11:1; Proverbs 11:25).

Get Ready for Action! Spiritual Warfare

1. We are a spiritual army

a. We are spiritual soldiers, fighting spiritual battles and sometimes must endure hardship (2 Timothy 2:3) as we help people some out of spiritual darkness.

b. Church is like an army with a medical unit—where God's soldiers receive healing and get back on battlefield.

c. We must encourage each other to stand strong as an army. Hebrews 3:13a

2. Prayer—A spiritual weapon to wage war

a. Put on the whole armor to wage war (Ephesians 6:10-12).

b. Prayer is a powerful weapon against the powers of darkness.

c. Satan blinds the minds of people who do not believe. 2 Corinthians 4:3-4a

d. We can bind the demonic strongholds in peoples' lives. Matthew 18:18

3. Truth keeps you grounded

a. The spiritual belt of truth stabilized the armor and weapons mentioned in Ephesians 6:13-14.

b. We must build everything in our lives on the truth of Jesus Christ.

4. **What coves your heart and feet?**
   a. The breastplate of righteousness (Ephesians 6:14b) causes us to see that we are righteous through faith in God. Romans 4:3-5
   b. We also must make sure our feet are fitted with the "readiness that comes from the gospel of peace." Ephesians 6:15
   c. We should attempt to live peaceably with all. James 3:18; Matthew 5:23-24; Romans 12:18

5. **Hold your shield of faith in place**
   a. The shield of faith is an overall defense against attack. Ephesians 6:16
   b. The fiery arrows of the enemy may include doubt, depression, condemnation, fear, etc.
   c. In faith, choose to speak forth the promises of God no matter what the circumstances.

   Ex: Mother continues to believe in faith for her wayward son (Isaiah 59:21b).

6. **Your helmet and sword**
   a. The helmet of salvation defends us from the blows of the enemy. The helmet give us hope of continual safety and protection (Ephesians 6:17a).
   b. The sword of the Spirit (the Word of God) is the only piece of armor that is offensive as well as defensive.
   c. Armed with the truth of God's Word, we can withstand Satan's lies.

7. **Ready for action!**
   a. We need to pray for each other to be bold in our witness. Ephesians 6:19-20
   b. Spiritual failure often happens when we fail to keep our spiritual armor in place.
   c. The world is waiting for us to declare the truth that will set them free!

Reaching the Lost and Making Disciples

1. True evangelism
 a. Evangelism is being so filled with Jesus that wherever we go, we discover people who need to know Him.
 b. Loving God is a call to love others (Luke 10:27).
 c. Jesus wants to make us fishers of men (Mark 1:17).

2. The *oikos* principle
 a. A great way to lead people to Christ is the oikos principle.
 b. *Oiko*s means *household or family*. They are the people we relate to on a regular basis.
 c. Cornelius invites his *oikos* to meet with Peter to hear the gospel (Acts 10:24).
 d. A jailor's entire household came to Christ in Acts 16.

3. Kinds of people in your *oikos*
 a. Family, relatives, neighbors, co-workers, and others with whom you have regular contact are a part of your oikos.
 b. Levi invites his oikos (business associates) to hear Jesus. Luke 5:29
 c. Philip's friendship with Nathanel brought him to Jesus. John 1:45

4. Spend time mentoring others

a. Jesus spent time with 12 disciples to mentor them. Mark 3:14-15

b. Making disciples is laying down our lives for others, taking the time needed to see them grow spiritually.

5. Learn and teach by example

a. We are called to train others. We have a responsibility to teach them what we ourselves have learned. Deuteronomy 29:29

b. If every disciple would train others, the results would be astounding.

6. Hospitality in homes

a. Hospitality is a powerful way of being involved in discipleship (1 Peter 4:9).

b. Romans 12:13 says we should "practice hospitality."

7. Sowing spiritual seeds in others' lives

a. Sow spiritual seeds in people's lives through prayer, encouragement, and discipleship.

b. What might happen when we sow spiritual seeds (Mark 4)?

c. Some hear God's Word, fail to respond, so Satan steals it away.

d. Some receive with gladness, but have shallow roots and die.

e. Some hear God's Word, believe and persevere. They will bear fruit (Mark 4:20).

f. The Great Commission is sowing seed.

You Are Called to Be a Spiritual Father or Mother!

1. The need for spiritual fathers and mothers

a. Spiritual parenting is for mentoring—developing and encouraging others to walk the path of becoming parents themselves.

b. Paul said the early church had teachers, but did not have enough of parents, true fathers and mothers, to give them a proper identity and nurturing (1 Corinthians 4:14-15).

2. God wants to "turn the hearts of the fathers to the children"

Malachi 4:6

a. Spiritual parents take up the mantle to train spiritual children and impart a legacy.

b. Paul trained Timothy and sent him to the Corinthians to train them (1 Corinthians 4:17).

c. This kind of mentoring relationship is a spiritual investment.

3. Spiritual children go through growth stages

1 John 2:12-14

a. Babies have to grow into young adults and then become parents.

b. Coming to a place of spiritual parenthood is the cry of God's heart.

c. If we remain spiritual babies, we fail to develop spiritually. Paul desired to properly ground people in the faith.
Colossians 1:28

4. Growing from spiritual children to young men and women

a. Spiritual babies are in fellowship with God (1 John 2:12) but are expected to grow spiritually.

b. Spiritual young men and women have learned how to apply God's Word (1 John 2:14). They are strong in the Word and Spirit (1 Timothy 4:12).

c. Spiritual young people still have growing to do, however.

5. Spiritual fathers and mothers defined

a. A spiritual young man or woman must grow up to become a parent by having children.

b. Spiritual parents have grown and matured (1 John 2:13).

c. A spiritual father or mothers helps a spiritual son or daughter reach his or her God-given potential.

6. Our inheritance of spiritual children

a. Like Abraham, we can have an inheritance of spiritual children and "birth" nations (Genesis 17:4; Galatians 3:29).

b. Make disciples by training a spiritual son or daughter!

7. Go into all the world and leave a legacy!

a. The promise of spiritual children is for every Christian.

b. Our inheritance will be the spiritual children we present to Christ (1 Thessalonians 2:19-20).

c. God uses the principle of multiplication through spiritual parenting to see God's kingdom advance.

d. Allow God to pour His Spirit on you to flow out to others! Acts 2:17

Chapter 1
What is the Great Commission?
Journaling space for reflection questions

DAY 1

What is a commission? Where are you called to make disciples?

① A co-operative mission with us acting co-operatively + corporately w/ God to Fulfill His set of orders + instructions ② Everywhere

DAY 2

Where are we commissioned to carry the gospel, according to Matthew 28:19? How can we practically obey the Lord to reach the world? ① Everywhere ② By going, praying, + sending.

DAY 3

How are disciples made? Think of your spheres of friendships; how can you make disciples within those spheres?

① One at a time. ② By walking closely with them + pouring the love of Christ + your life into them.

DAY 4

Why is a small group a more effective setting for discipling than a larger group? (1) Because you can build family type relationships in small settings.

DAY 5

Who should we imitate (1 Corinthians 11:1)? Describe a time you saw Christ in someone and it influenced your life. (1) Other strong followers who can mentor us in the faith as they + subsequently we walk out the faith immitating Christ. (2) When I saw my bro. Bob come back from Brazil after he had been broken + then restored, renewed by Christ.

DAY 6

What do you think the spotless bride of Christ will look like? Unified, purified, harmonized

DAY 7

When we pour our lives out for others, what are we promised in Luke 6:38? In Proverbs 11:25? (1) A bounty worth of reaping. What we pour out + into will be poured back out + into us in proportion to His abundance, greatness + ability. (2) refreshment.

Chapter 2
Get Ready for Action!
Spiritual Warfare
Journaling space for reflection questions

DAY 1

How often should we encourage each other,
according to Hebrews 3:13? How do you encourage others?

① daily ② Words of edification, prayer, with
helping them (if the chance arises + I am able)
words of scripture.

DAY 2

How do we stand against Satan's schemes (Ephesians 6:10-12)?

① By being read up, prayed up + living it up
putting on the full armor of God.

DAY 3

In what ways does the devil attempt to knock you off your feet
and make you ineffective in battle? How does God's Word, His
truth, keep you stable? ① by wrecking your moral
thru emotions + circumstance.
② Simply because it is true +
eternally true where as a circumstance or
emotion may be real it is temporal.

How do we obtain righteousness? How can you be a peacemaker? Explain. ① by Faith in Jesus Christ. ② By pursuing peace.

How do we defend ourselves from Satan's "flaming arrows"?
① By our shield of Faith.

How does the helmet of salvation help us fight the battle?
Why is the sword of the Spirit so important? ① The shear knowledge that our salvation comes from God + our acceptance of Christ + His (not only willingness) but desire to do so should give us great comfort. ② It is the truth, The word of God our defense against lies + liars.

When we pour our lives out for others, what are we promised in Luke 6:38? In Proverbs 11:25?

Huh??

I have the Full
armor   belt - truth
          breast plate - righteousness
          shield - Faith
          helmet - Salvation
          Sword - of the Spirit

The Great Commission

Chapter 3
Reaching the Lost
and Making Disciples
Journaling space for reflection questions

What does evangelism mean to you? How did Jesus evangelize?

It means to enlighten people + to make a formal introduction to the Creator + lover of their soul + then to instigate several more chance (not really - yet divine appointments) nurturing the relationship, hoping their eyes open to enlightenment. ① By relating to them on a level they can understand + relate to + healing them when + where they need it most.

What does "oikos" mean? List people in your oikos.

① My immediate area of influence.

② My family, my brides friends, my friends, my sub contractors, the store, my customers,

Explain how you have released your faith in the past week.

① I loved on the "little of faith" by going to the relatives "showing" bearing gifts along with Ivy my beautiful wife, giving comfort + healing

List some practical ways we can make ourselves available to train disciples. ① Model the truth ② Reach out for companionship. ③ Care for them as friends + train them to grow in their Christian faith. ④ Pray with them ⑤ encourage them ⑥ Help them focus on the word of God + Christ Himself.

What are we responsible for, according to Deuteronomy 29:29? How can we pass on what we have learned to others?

① To act on those things revealed to us by God.

② By discipling others teaching them to go out + make disciples.

What does hospitality mean to you? How should we offer hospitality, according to 1 Peter 4:9? ① Grace, welcomeness, to bring comfort to others, to invite others to drawl in closer to us, to shelter, protect, & comfort + host hospitabably.

② w/out grumbling.

How do you sow spiritual seeds? In faith
What does faith have to do with planting seeds in others' lives?

① Through prayer, the word, encouraging making disciples by reaching the lost — In faith.

② We are expectant knowing God's word will not return to Him void —

AMEN !!

Chapter 4
You Are Called to Be
a Spiritual Father or Mother
Journaling space for reflection questions

Why were the Christians immature in 1 Corinthians 4:14-15?
Do you sense a need for a spiritual father or mother to equip you
to "go into the world"? Are you willing to become a spiritual father
or mother?

① They didn't have spiritual
parenting. ② I have them thankyou.
③ When God, my spiritual parents, + I
believe I am equipped + mature enough to do
so,

Why is it important for spiritual parents to take up the mantle and
train their children? What happens when spiritual sons and
daughters are mentored and equipped by spiritual parents?

① So that it will spread + pass on for generation
of spiritual children + not be lost,
② It becomes modeled + multiplys,

What are the growth stages for a new Christian to become a
spiritual parent himself?
What happens if we fail to go through these stages?

① little children, young men, fathers
② We remain babes, or fall away.

What are some characteristics of spiritual children? Of spiritual young men and women? ① Immaturity, instability, gullibility

② Strong in Word, disciplined in spirit, alive, mature, yet arrogant & dogmatic.

How do spiritual young men and women become parents? Give a definition of a spiritual father or mother.

① By having children.
② Those mature & strong in the faith that have an ongoing intimate relationship with Christ & are changing daily to be more & more like Him.

How can we birth a spiritual lineage according to Galatians 3:29?

By reproducing a prodigy & heir in the Kingdom of God & teaching them (our children) to be mature & be fruitful also.

What is our spiritual legacy? How does having and becoming a spiritual parent help you obey the Great Commission?

Our spiritual prodigies. Making disciples of all the nations. By exponential training to train, to train etc. . . .

Coordinates with this series!

Biblical Foundations for Children

Creative learning experiences for ages 4-12, patterned after the *Biblical Foundation Series*, with truths in each lesson. Takes kids on the first steps in their Christian walk by teaching them how to build solid foundations in their young lives. *by Jane Nicholas, 176 pages:* $17.95

Other books by Larry Kreider

Hearing God 30 Different ways

The Lord speaks to us in ways we often miss. He has many ways of speaking, including through the Bible, prayer, circumstances, spiritual gifts, conviction, His character, His peace, and even in times of silence.

30 ways in 30 days Take the next 30 days, reading a chapter each day, to explore ways God speaks. Expect to be surprised! Use as a personal devotional or go through this material with your small group or congregation. *by Larry Kreider, 224 pages:* $14.99

The Cry for Spiritual Fathers & Mothers

Returning to the biblical truth of spiritual parenting so believers are not left fatherless and disconnected. How loving, seasoned spiritual fathers and mothers help spiritual children reach their full potential in Christ. *by Larry Kreider, 186 pages*: $11.95

The Biblical Role of Elders for Today's Church

New Testament leadership principles for equipping elders. What elders' qualifications and responsibilities are, how they are chosen, how elders are called to be armor bearers, spiritual fathers and mothers, resolving conflicts, and more. *by Larry Kreider, Ron Myer, Steve Prokopchak, and Brian Sauder.* $12.99

Visit www.dcfi.org for more information